This journal
belongs to:

_____

THE
Self-Care
Prescription
Journal

**Powerful Prompts to Manage
Emotions, Cultivate Well-Being,
and Achieve Your Goals**

Robyn L. Gobin, PhD

ROCKRIDGE
PRESS

For Daddy, Mama, and "J." You set the foundation for the woman I am today. I hope I'm making you proud.

For general information on our other products and services or to obtain technical support, please contact our Customer Care Department within the United States at (866) 744-2665, or outside the United States at (510) 253-0500.

Interior and Cover Designer: Mando Daniel
Art Producer: Tom Hood
Editors: Carolyn Abate and Nora Spiegel
Production Editor: Matthew Burnett
Production Manager: Michael Kay

Cover illustration © iStock, 2021.

Author photograph: Korey Gobin

ISBN: Print 978-1-64876-678-7

R0

Contents

Introduction:
Why You Need Self-Care

Imagine if everyone took good care of themselves. What would this world look like? In my vision, people would set boundaries and say no when necessary, have difficult conversations, speak up (even when afraid), engage in soul-nourishing movement, sleep eight hours every night, sit with difficult emotions, treat themselves kindly, rise above adversity, forgive themselves as freely as they forgive others, and embrace their imperfections. Yes, there would be the occasional pedicure and exotic vacation, but in my ideal world, self-care would be a daily lifestyle, not an occasional luxury. People would realize they deserve to take care of themselves and wouldn't let other people's disapproval get in the way. If feelings of guilt arose, they would have the courage to persist in self-care as an act of self-love.

Looking at the world now, my dream might seem a bit unrealistic. Our fast-paced society and impractical standards have morphed us into human *doings*—constantly on the go, juggling multiple responsibilities, being everything to everybody but ourselves. Like hamsters on a wheel, we keep spinning and spinning. We've accepted sleep deficiency as the norm. Our lives have become imbalanced as we spend energy on things that don't matter, and we've lost sight of the people who do. For those from marginalized backgrounds, self-sacrifice to the point of utter depletion seems necessary for survival. While this superhuman way of existing has helped us survive, it has come at a cost, leaving some of us tired, overwhelmed, dissatisfied, and resentful.

I say it's time we pump the breaks. We can resist the impulse to function on "high" all the time. We can create more balance and the space to breathe and just be. Self-care doesn't just benefit us as individuals; it also benefits our communities. We are all too familiar with social injustices and how they negatively affect people with marginalized identities. I believe we can create a kinder and more caring world, but we have to be well—in body, mind, and spirit. Self-care is about tending to your needs so you have the energy and creativity to fight for positive change in the world around you.

How much better would your life be if you honored your limitations and took time to rest? What would be possible if you tended to your own needs with the same energy that you tend to everyone else's? Wouldn't it be amazing to give the best of yourself to the people and things that matter most?

I created this journal as a companion to my 2019 book, *The Self-Care Prescription*. Think of it as a tool to help you make intentional choices that lead you to feel alive, cared for, and inspired. If we're going to make changes, we need space for self-reflection so we can see how we want or need to change and how best to do it.

In this journal, you will find prompts that allow you to reflect on your current level of self-care so that you can see which habits and patterns are working for you and which ones are not. With increased awareness comes the possibility of change. The journal prompts have been specially curated to allow you to see you see what's possible and identify the steps necessary to take your self-care to the next level. You'll find prompts encouraging you to take inspired actions, closing the gap between where you are and where you want to be on your self-care journey. Most importantly, the prompts remind you that you always have a choice when it comes to self-care. No matter what you've experienced in the past or what the future holds, I want you to feel empowered to tend to your needs.

The sections in this journal are structured around the six domains of wellness:

- Social: the quality of your relationships and play

- Physical: nutrition, sleep/rest, movement, and body awareness

- Intellectual: mental stimulation

- Vocational: Meaningful work and a balance between work and personal life

- Spiritual: broader connections and purpose

- Emotional: understanding, expressing, and coping with emotions and stress

I designed the journal this way so you can honor all your needs. Too often our lives fall out of balance as one area of life gets all of our attention. I recommend taking one section of this journal at a time and giving focused attention to that area of self-care. Remember, the ultimate goal of awareness is behavioral change; that's why I have included plenty of space to write down your self-care thoughts, ideas, and plans. Once you identify which areas need care and the best next steps to take, I want you to join me in making my vision a reality, one small step at time. This will be a marathon, not a sprint. To give you the motivation to keep going, I've included tips throughout each domain. As with any journey, you'll likely encounter barriers and challenges along the way. Be flexible, but whatever you do, don't stop showing up for yourself. I truly believe that together we can create a world where self-care is not the exception but the standard.

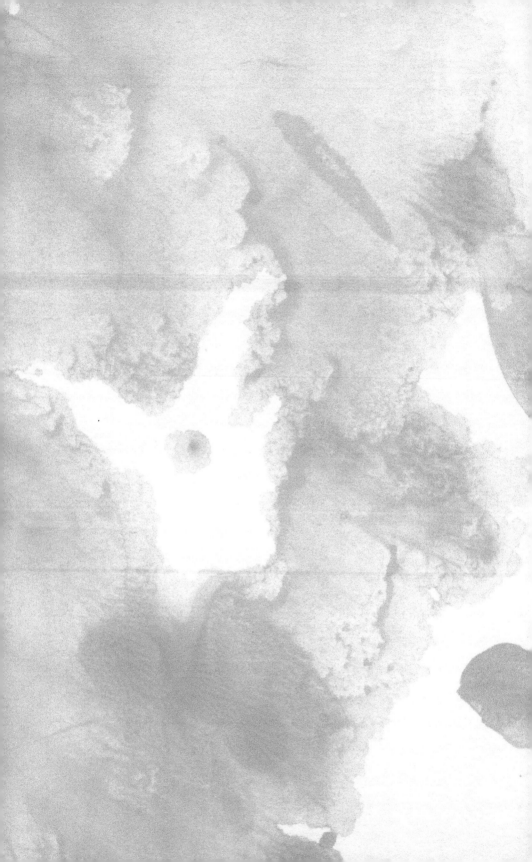

Social Self-Care

We were not meant to do life alone. Social self-care involves tending to your need for connection with others, whether that's by creating new connections or by nurturing established relationships. Social self-care also involves making time for hobbies, recreation, and play. We take care of ourselves socially when we purposefully create lighthearted moments, make time for the people (and pets!) we care about, and build strong bonds through transparent communication, frequent interaction, and mutual investment of emotional energy. Practically speaking, social self-care involves regularly scheduling activities with the people you love, being fully present and engaged when you're with them, staying open to new relationships, and keeping in touch with friends and loved ones who don't live nearby.

Although social self-care can be fulfilling and enjoyable, it can also be uncomfortable. Sometimes it requires that we set boundaries, have difficult conversations, or let go of unhealthy relationships, which can be especially difficult to do.

As our lives grow busier and we take on more responsibilities, it's easy to put relationships on the back burner. Some of us have developed habits of isolating ourselves when life gets difficult, especially if we're from marginalized groups and feel we can't rely on others. Despite these challenges, prioritizing social self-care is worth the effort. Strong social connections can decrease your vulnerability to physical illness and poor mental health and allow for a longer, more enjoyable life. The prompts in this section will help you explore where you are now in terms of social self-care, identify changes you want to make, and develop plans for enhancing this area of your life.

On a scale from 0 to 10 where 0 is completely dissatisfied and 10 is completely satisfied, how satisfied are you with your social life? What is one thing you would change about it? What small step can you take in the next week to improve, enhance, or revive your social life?

_____

_____

_____

_____

_____

_____

_____

_____

_____

_____

_____

_____

_____

_____

_____

_____

_____

_____

_____

It is important that we feel loved, valued, fully accepted, and supported in our relationships. Who loves, values, fully accepts, and supports you? Reach out to one of these people today by text, email, or phone, and express your gratitude for their love and support. What was their response? How did it feel to receive this response?

_____

_____

_____

_____

_____

_____

_____

_____

_____

_____

_____

_____

_____

_____

_____

_____

Self-care helps you show up authentically in your relationships.

Maya Angelou wrote, "I've learned that people will forget what you said, people will forget what you did, but people will never forget how you made them feel." Think about the people you are in relationships with. How do you want to make them feel? What can you do or say to accomplish this? How can taking better care of yourself help you show up more fully for others?

_____

_____

_____

_____

_____

_____

_____

_____

_____

_____

_____

_____

_____

_____

_____

_____

_____

_____

We sometimes silence ourselves in relationships for the sake of keeping the peace. Although our silence minimizes friction, it can also create a barrier to deeper understanding and connection. How have you silenced yourself in your relationships with others? What has your silence cost you?

_____

_____

_____

_____

_____

_____

_____

_____

_____

_____

_____

_____

_____

_____

_____

_____

_____

Prioritize the people who genuinely accept you and add value to your life.

Which relationships are draining you right now? Boundary setting is crucial to avoiding burnout and can be done in a gentle and respectful way. Setting boundaries means letting people know what you need, like, and dislike. You can set boundaries around how you want to be treated and how you want to communicate. What is one relationship that could use some healthy boundaries? What might those boundaries look like?

_____

_____

_____

_____

_____

_____

_____

_____

_____

_____

_____

_____

_____

_____

_____

_____

Because we are all imperfect, when we are in close relationships with other people, sooner or later we are bound to unintentionally offend them or fall short of their expectations. What imperfect moments have you had in your relationships? Are you quick to cut other people off when they have human moments? How can you extend more grace to yourself and others?

_____

_____

_____

_____

_____

_____

_____

_____

_____

_____

_____

_____

_____

_____

_____

_____

_____

_____

Your social network is the people you choose to spend time with because you have things in common, share similar values, enjoy each other's company, and add value to each other's lives. Who is in your social network? How do they add value to your life? If you haven't found your social network, what kinds of relationships would be most meaningful to you? What things do you enjoy that you'd like to do with others?

_____

_____

_____

_____

_____

_____

_____

_____

_____

_____

_____

_____

_____

_____

_____

_____

_____

_____

Joy is a feeling of pleasure that's independent of external circumstances. Joy is a choice, an attitude that stems from inner hope, peace, and contentment. When do you feel most joyful? What are some intentional ways you can create more joy in your life?

_____

_____

_____

_____

_____

_____

_____

_____

_____

_____

_____

_____

_____

_____

_____

_____

Let go of the things and people that no longer serve you so there is more space for love, joy, and growth.

One of the greatest gifts you can give the people you love is your undivided attention. How can you engage more fully in your relationships? How can you be more intentional about spending quality, distraction-free time with the people you love?

_____

_____

_____

_____

_____

_____

_____

_____

_____

_____

_____

_____

_____

_____

_____

_____

_____

_____

_____

_____

_____

_____

Receiving help is one aspect of healthy relationships that makes us feel close and connected. Asking for help is an act of self-care, but it doesn't always come easily. How do you feel about asking for help? What barriers keep you from asking for help when you need it?

_____

_____

_____

_____

_____

_____

_____

_____

_____

_____

_____

_____

_____

_____

_____

_____

_____

Although it can be uncomfortable and scary, being vulnerable in a relationship helps you get your needs met while making you feel more connected, supported, and understood. What feelings do you hide from others? What hard conversations have you been putting off?

_____

_____

_____

_____

_____

_____

_____

_____

_____

_____

_____

_____

_____

_____

_____

_____

_____

_____

_____

Everyone has different preferences regarding how they spend time with others—how often they get together, where they meet, and what they do. Some people enjoy pure small talk, while others prefer to socialize during activities like playing games, dancing, or working toward a shared goal. What do you enjoy doing most in social settings? How do your preferences vary based on who you are spending time with?

_____

_____

_____

_____

_____

_____

_____

_____

_____

_____

_____

_____

_____

_____

_____

_____

Start small with your social self-care routine. Small changes have a big impact over time.

When we have been hurt or betrayed in the past, sometimes we try to protect ourselves from future hurt by keeping new people at a distance. We put up walls by testing their loyalty or trustworthiness and push them away when they get too close. We may also refrain from sharing intimate details or showing emotions. What emotional walls do you put up in new relationships? How do they protect and harm you?

We've likely all heard the saying "Friendships are a two-way street." I recently came across a meme that said, "Friendship is like a bank account; you cannot continue to withdraw from it without making deposits." Thinking about your current relationships, is there a balance between withdrawals and deposits? If an imbalance exists, what is one step you can take to bring it more into balance?

_____

_____

_____

_____

_____

_____

_____

_____

_____

_____

_____

_____

_____

_____

_____

_____

_____

_____

Forgiveness is something you do for yourself to release the mental and emotional bondage of holding on to negative feelings and pain. It allows you to move forward and avoid sabotaging new relationships with old baggage and expectations. Forgiveness is a process. Who do you need to forgive? What is one step you can take today toward forgiveness?

_____

_____

_____

_____

_____

_____

_____

_____

_____

_____

_____

_____

_____

_____

_____

_____

_____

_____

_____

Sometimes self-care involves nurturing our existing relationships. Other times, it looks like creating new social connections.
What is missing in your social life? What social needs do you
have that are not currently being fulfilled? What interest or
activity would you like to build new connections around?

_____

_____

_____

_____

_____

_____

_____

_____

_____

_____

_____

_____

_____

_____

_____

*Social self-care requires intentionality.
You have the power to create the relationships
you desire.*

If you're like most adults, you could probably use more play in your life. Play can be a great stress reliever and can enhance creativity and innovation. It can include anything: a scavenger hunt, hiking, dancing, playing board games or cards, or going to a haunted house with friends on Halloween. What are some new fun things you'd like to try? How you can incorporate new ways to play into your routine?

Imagine you could be friends with any public figure: your favorite actor, musician, celebrity, social media personality, reality television star, author, a politician, the president, or a business or brand leader. Who would you want to be friends with? What qualities do you believe this person would bring to the relationship? In what ways do you think they would support you or help you reach your goals in life?

_____

_____

_____

_____

_____

_____

_____

_____

_____

_____

_____

Create balance between joy and rest in your life. Joy is lively and exuberant, while rest is easy and relaxed. Both are essential to your self-care.

Self-advocacy is a lovely act of self-care. When we advocate for ourselves, we ask for what we need clearly and directly. Would you describe yourself as a good self-advocate? Why or why not? What is one way you can improve your self-advocacy skills?

Knowing your social needs requires taking time to quiet the outside noise and connect with yourself. One of the best ways to do that is to disconnect from social media. Have you ever taken a break from social media? If so, how did it help you connect with your own needs, desires, and inner wisdom? If not, how could taking a break from social media be beneficial?

_____

_____

_____

_____

_____

_____

_____

_____

_____

_____

_____

_____

_____

_____

_____

_____

_____

_____

No matter how close you are to the people you love, differences of opinion and disagreements are bound to occur. What is your go-to strategy for dealing with conflict? How comfortable are you working through disagreements with friends, partners, or family members? Are you afraid to disagree with someone you love?

_____

_____

_____

_____

_____

_____

_____

_____

_____

_____

_____

_____

_____

_____

_____

_____

_____

_____

_____

Are there any friends you have lost touch with due to geo-graphic distance or just life in general? What are some ways that you can reconnect and revive those old friendships?

_____

_____

_____

_____

_____

_____

_____

_____

_____

_____

_____

_____

_____

_____

_____

_____

_____

_____

_____

Schedule social time in your calendar and make it nonnegotiable.

Our society places a ton of unrealistic expectations on how we should look, think, and behave. These expectations vary based on factors like sex at birth, age, ethnic identity, gender identity, ability status, sexual orientation, socioeconomic background, and more. How have society's rigid labels and standards affected your relationships?

_____

_____

_____

_____

_____

_____

_____

_____

_____

_____

_____

_____

_____

_____

_____

_____

_____

_____

_____

When we face the challenges of life, whether they be personal failures, disappointments, or unexpected loss, we all need soft places to land, places where we can be our authentic selves and express the pain we feel without fear of judgment. Where are these places for you? When do you feel seen and heard the most?

_____

_____

_____

_____

_____

_____

_____

_____

_____

_____

_____

_____

_____

_____

_____

_____

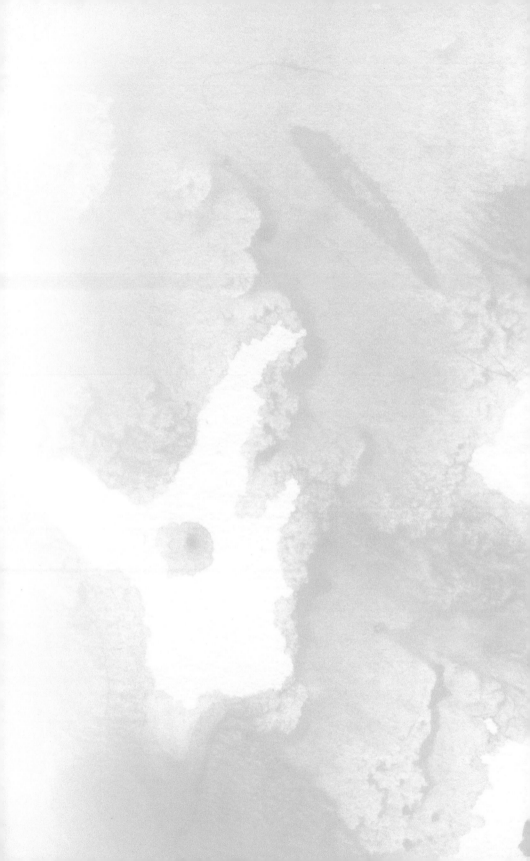

Physical Self-Care

Physical self-care refers to activities you engage in to take care of your body. Traditionally, we think about physical self-care as having three main components: movement, sleep/rest, and food/nutrition. All three are necessary aspects of physical self-care that work together to keep our bodies healthy and functioning to the best of their ability.

Movement includes how you enjoy moving your body, and the activities that you engage in to keep your body healthy and strong. Sleep and rest give your body time to recharge, relax, and replenish. And food/nutrition, of course, is the way you energize and nourish your body; your relationship with food and eating is also relevant. I would argue that there is an equally important fourth component: your relationship with your body. This includes how you view, touch, talk about, and care for your body. Your body relationship is central to physical self-care because the way you relate to your body will determine how you take care of it. The more intimate your body relationship, the better you'll be at giving your body the specific care it needs.

It is essential that we prioritize physical self-care. As the saying goes, "If you take care of your body, it will take care of you." When we neglect physical self-care, we are more vulnerable to disease, exhaustion, and injuries. We take for granted daily activities like sitting up, walking, running, staring at screens for hours, and standing for long periods. Our bodies work for us nonstop. Physical self-care is the compensation we give our bodies for that labor.

When beginning any new journey, it is important to identify your "why," your sense of purpose. Having your "why" written down will help you remember why physical self-care is important to you and help you prioritize it when other demands vie for your time and attention. Why is physical self-care important to you? What goals do you hope it will help you achieve?

_____

_____

_____

_____

_____

_____

_____

_____

_____

_____

_____

_____

_____

_____

_____

_____

_____

We can control some aspects of physical self-care, like how often we move; but other aspects, like the family we were born into and the medical history we've inherited, are beyond our control. Does your family have a history of serious illness or disease? How has this history impacted your approach to physical self-care?

_____

_____

_____

_____

_____

_____

_____

_____

_____

_____

_____

_____

You are not required to be perfect or in control of everything when it comes to self-care. Focus on the things that are in your power to control.

Regular medical checkups are important because they increase your body knowledge and can help you catch problems before they become life-threatening. When was the last time you had a physical or medical checkup? Do you see your doctor regularly? Why or why not?

_____

_____

_____

_____

_____

_____

_____

_____

_____

_____

_____

_____

_____

_____

_____

_____

_____

_____

When you become aware of physical pain or any unusual symptoms in your body, how do you respond? Do you avoid going to the doctor? Some people avoid medical professionals because they are afraid of receiving bad news or having their pain dismissed or downplayed. How have your past experiences with healthcare professionals affected your willingness to seek medical care when you need it?

_____

_____

_____

_____

_____

_____

_____

_____

_____

_____

_____

_____

_____

Listening to the messages your body gives you the first time around prevents a minor alarm from turning into a major crisis.

What experience do you have with medication, and how do you feel about it? Some beliefs about medication make it difficult to consistently take it as prescribed. Have you struggled with this?

_____

_____

_____

_____

_____

_____

_____

_____

_____

_____

_____

_____

_____

_____

_____

_____

_____

_____

_____

_____

Moving your body regularly has several benefits. It can boost your mood, increase energy, and help prevent or manage chronic health conditions. What types of movement do you enjoy? What steps can you take to more regularly engage in movement you enjoy?

_____

_____

_____

_____

_____

_____

_____

_____

_____

_____

_____

_____

_____

_____

_____

Food can be a source of nourishment, pleasure, and satisfaction. How often do you allow yourself to eat for pleasure or satisfaction? Do you regularly deprive yourself of certain foods? What emotions do you most commonly experience before, during, and after eating?

_____

_____

_____

_____

_____

_____

_____

_____

_____

_____

_____

_____

_____

_____

_____

_____

_____

_____

Water enables your body to run well.

When it comes to weight and our bodies, we can be our own worst critic. In what ways do you judge or criticize your body? How does this make you feel? How do your beliefs about your body impact your choices and behaviors? How can you become more positive toward your body?

_____

_____

_____

_____

_____

_____

_____

_____

_____

_____

_____

_____

_____

_____

_____

_____

_____

_____

Rather than punishment or an agonizing chore, movement should feel fun, empowering, and adventurous. Would you consider yourself an adventurous person? Regardless of your answer, how might you bring an attitude of fun and adventure into your movement practices?

For optimal wellness, the American Academy of Sleep Medicine and Sleep Research Society recommends seven or more hours of sleep per night for adults. Sleeping less than that is associated with a host of negative, sometimes deadly, consequences. What prevents you from consistently getting seven or more hours of sleep per night? If you get enough sleep, what benefits (health and otherwise) have you noticed?

_____

_____

_____

_____

_____

_____

_____

_____

_____

_____

_____

_____

_____

_____

_____

_____

Our bodies need rest to refuel and recover from the demands we place on them. There are many ways to rest. In her book *Sacred Rest*, Dr. Saundra Dalton-Smith describes seven types: physical (keep blood circulating), mental (calm the mind), emotional (accept emotions), spiritual (connect beyond the mental and physical), social (surround yourself with positive relationships), sensory (reduce overstimulation), and creative (appreciate beauty around you). How often do you rest? Of the seven types of rest, which one is your body most in need of?

_____

_____

_____

_____

_____

_____

_____

_____

_____

_____

_____

_____

_____

_____

_____

_____

_____

Self-soothing is the ability to comfort, nurture, please, and be kind to your body. It's a great way to take care of yourself when you're in pain or feeling the weight of stress. It's fine to look to others for comfort, but it is also important to know how to soothe yourself. How frequently do you soothe your body? What are some ways you can do so?

_____

_____

_____

_____

_____

_____

_____

_____

_____

_____

_____

_____

Rest and sleep are related but different. Rest involves intentionally setting aside time to simply "be." It's like giving your body a positive, restorative time-out.

The clothing we wear can have an impact on how we feel about our bodies. Clothes that make you feel comfortable, attractive, and confident can positively affect your mental health and body image. What types of clothing make you feel best? What makes you feel attractive?

_____

_____

_____

_____

_____

_____

_____

_____

_____

_____

_____

_____

_____

_____

_____

_____

_____

_____

_____

_____

When your body tells you it's had enough, do you listen? If you're like most Americans, you probably push your body past its limits. Our society's obsession with productivity and achievement causes us to dismiss the signals our bodies give us to slow down. How do you respond when your body makes you aware of any limitations?

_____

_____

_____

_____

_____

_____

_____

_____

_____

_____

_____

_____

_____

_____

_____

_____

_____

_____

_____

Body-shaming, or humiliating someone with comments about their body shape or size, can start at a young age and continue throughout our lives as we are bombarded with messages from media, society, and family and friends that tell us our bodies are unacceptable. Have you experienced body-shaming, either from others or yourself? What impact has body-shaming had on your physical self-care?

_____

_____

_____

_____

_____

_____

_____

_____

_____

_____

_____

_____

_____

_____

_____

_____

_____

_____

Your body doesn't need to change for you to be happy, acceptable, worthy, and attractive.

Do you freely take up physical space in your daily life? Some people, especially those with marginalized identities, are discouraged from taking up space with their bodies or words. According to television producer Shonda Rhimes, the remedy is to decide that you belong: "Plenty of people will decide that this room is not for you to be in. Your only job is for you to decide that every room you are in is a room that you belong in, and to remain there. And, once you're there, you're good to go." How can you challenge yourself to take up more space in your day-to-day life?

_____

_____

_____

_____

_____

_____

_____

_____

_____

_____

_____

_____

_____

_____

_____

Growing up, when someone was moving fast and clumsily, my grandmother would say they were "running around like a chicken with its head cut off." We are often hurried in our lives, rushing from task to task without taking a moment to catch our breath. Slowing down can help us soak in the good moments and intentionally invest our energy in activities we find important. If I were to see you in your daily life, would I see someone who looks like a chicken with its head cut off? What is the speed of your life?

_____

_____

_____

_____

_____

_____

_____

_____

_____

_____

_____

Avoid overbooking your schedule and give yourself plenty of time between appointments. Build natural pauses and breaks throughout your day.

It's helpful to have a bedtime routine that signals to your body it's time to wind down and go to sleep. Bedtime routines are most effective when they are regular and around the same time each night. What is your routine? Is it working well for you? If you don't have a routine or if your current routine isn't working, how can you improve it?

_____

_____

_____

_____

_____

_____

_____

_____

_____

_____

_____

_____

_____

_____

_____

_____

_____

It's easy to get stuck in a rut moving your body in the same way over and over, but variety makes movement enjoyable and challenges our muscles in new ways. When was the last time you tried a new style of movement? Here are some ideas: dance, swim, plant a garden, walk in nature, or try an online yoga class. Which new form of movement are you willing to try at least once over the next week?

_____

_____

_____

_____

_____

_____

_____

_____

_____

_____

_____

_____

_____

_____

_____

_____

_____

_____

_____

Just because we want to regularly practice self-care doesn't mean it's easy. Each person has a unique set of barriers that can get in the way of physical self-care. These barriers can be motivational (e.g., dread certain types of movement), logistical (e.g., not enough time to exercise), financial (e.g., not enough money for equipment), physical (e.g., chronic pain or body aches), or mental or emotional (e.g., feeling insecure about your body). What are your personal barriers? List steps you can take to overcome one of the barriers you identified.

Mindful eating involves paying attention to what you are eating and how you are eating it as well as withholding judgment about certain foods as "good" or "bad." Eating mindfully involves six qualities: eating at a leisurely pace; observing the food's effect on your body, thoughts, and emotions; minimizing distractions; engaging all five senses; staying open-minded; and being kind to yourself when painful thoughts or emotions arise. Which quality do you believe would be the easiest for you to practice? Which would be the most challenging?

_____

_____

_____

_____

_____

_____

_____

_____

_____

_____

_____

_____

_____

_____

_____

_____

Eating regular, balanced meals helps give your body the nutrients it needs to do all the things you want it to do and protects it from illness and fatigue. One way to make sure you eat regularly is to plan your meals in advance. How can you plan more balanced, regular meals into your week?

_____

_____

_____

_____

_____

_____

_____

_____

_____

_____

_____

_____

_____

_____

_____

_____

_____

It can be fun to connect with others who share similar physical self-care values. You can think of them as your physical self-care support system—people who motivate and inspire you along your self-care journey. Your support system might include people who belong to the same gym, friends who you regularly walk with, or a partner who reminds you not to skip meals. Who is in your physical self-care support system? Are there types of support you would benefit from that you are not currently receiving?

_____

_____

_____

_____

_____

_____

_____

_____

_____

_____

_____

_____

_____

_____

_____

_____

For some strange reason, pleasure has gotten a bad reputation in our society, but we all deserve to feel happy, satisfied, and joyful. What is your relationship to pleasure? What experiences do you find pleasurable? How do you know when you are experiencing it? Where do you feel it in your body?

_____

_____

_____

_____

_____

_____

_____

_____

_____

_____

_____

_____

_____

Think creatively about meeting your physical self-care needs. Seemingly impossible situations usually have solutions if we consider the possibilities.

Intellectual Self-Care

Intellectual self-care involves actions that help your brain perform at its best—exercise for your mind. When we engage in intellectual self-care, we stimulate our minds, expand our knowledge, widen our perspectives, deepen our creativity, and indulge our curiosity.

Intellectual self-care can be as creative, expansive, and engaging as you want it to be. It can involve DIY projects, watching movies, listening to podcasts, visiting museums, various forms of artistic expression, and so much more. The key to flourishing in this area of self-care is to not limit yourself by buying into the idea that there is only one way to take care of your mind.

Our brains complete important functions, like retaining valuable skills and knowledge, coordinating simple and complex movements, storing a lifetime of memories, communicating sensory information, processing emotions, solving complex problems, expressing our creativity, and sensing connection to our loved ones. Our brains also allow us to think critically about current events and advocate for the causes we're passionate about in articulate and compelling ways. When you stop and think about it, our brains are miraculous. We rely heavily on them for virtually everything. Given this dependence, we would be wise to take good care of our brains by focusing on three important domains: building knowledge, engaging curiosity, and cultivating creativity. Practicing intellectual self-care can contribute to our overall health and happiness by expanding our ability to face old challenges in new and exciting ways.

Every day, our brains enable us to create, think critically, under-stand, remember, concentrate, cooperate, plan, and read and comprehend new information. Of all the ways your brain works for you, which one function do you most appreciate? Why? How would your life be more challenging if you did not have this ability?

_____

_____

_____

_____

_____

_____

_____

_____

_____

_____

_____

_____

_____

_____

_____

_____

_____

Reading for fun nourishes our brain by sparking creativity and helping us think about things we don't typically think about. When was the last time you read for the pure joy of reading, allowing yourself to get lost in the story? What is your favorite "just for fun" book? Why?

_____

_____

_____

_____

_____

_____

_____

_____

_____

_____

_____

_____

_____

_____

_____

_____

We know physical activity is great for the body, but did you also know that it benefits the brain? Yep! Activities like walking, hiking, running, and biking increase blood flow to the brain. What types of physical activity can you add into your weekly routine to give your brain a boost?

_____

_____

_____

_____

_____

_____

_____

_____

_____

_____

_____

_____

_____

_____

_____

_____

_____

_____

_____

_____

Considering perspectives that differ from your own is a great way to stimulate critical thinking and improve your ability to make wise decisions. What activities can you engage in to broaden your perspective?

_____

_____

_____

_____

_____

_____

_____

_____

_____

_____

_____

_____

_____

_____

_____

_____

Mix up your routine to keep your mind sharp.

When you want to learn something new, it is important to set goals for yourself. Establishing goals sets you up for success by helping you identify your priorities and action steps. Goals are most effective when they are SMART:

Specific—clearly stated

Measurable—quantified so that you can determine whether you met them

Achievable—realistic, given your time and energy

Relevant—meet a specific need

Time-bound—have a clear beginning and end

Practice setting an intellectual self-care SMART goal. How does breaking down your goal in this way feel?

_____

_____

_____

_____

_____

_____

_____

_____

_____

_____

_____

We remember new information and perform new skills best when we are curious about the subject. When was the last time you learned something that you were actually hungry to know? How was that experience different than learning about something you weren't interested in?

_____

_____

_____

_____

_____

_____

_____

_____

_____

_____

_____

_____

_____

_____

_____

_____

_____

Our brains don't function to the best of their ability when we don't get enough sleep. On a 0 - 10 scale where 0 is the worst sleep possible and 10 is the best, how would you rate the quality of your sleep? What are three things you can do to ensure you get the best sleep possible?

_____

_____

_____

_____

_____

_____

_____

_____

_____

_____

_____

_____

_____

_____

_____

_____

_____

_____

_____

One general benefit to learning a new language is that it helps keep your mind sharp. If you could learn a new language, which one would you choose? How would learning it benefit you? What would the new language skills make possible?

_____

_____

_____

_____

_____

_____

_____

_____

_____

_____

_____

_____

_____

_____

_____

_____

Learning new things is challenging and takes time to master. Be patient and kind with yourself as you are learning new skills.

Watch a TED Talk. Write down the key points you learned. How can you apply this new knowledge to your life?

_____

_____

_____

_____

_____

_____

_____

_____

_____

_____

_____

_____

_____

_____

_____

_____

_____

_____

_____

_____

When you were little, what types of games did you like to play? How did these games challenge your mind intellectually? What games do you enjoy playing as an adult?

_____

_____

_____

_____

_____

_____

_____

_____

_____

_____

_____

_____

_____

_____

_____

_____

_____

_____

_____

There are countless ways to be creative. Playing music, painting, repurposing old furniture, reconfiguring a room in your home, exploring local, new-to-you attractions where you live, photography, journaling, meditating, creating a Pinterest board, trying a new recipe, taking an art class, trying your hand at improv or acting, or taking up a new DIY project are just a few options. How can you infuse more creativity into your life this week?

Trying new things keeps our brains sharp by creating space for new information that can be stored and accessed later when we need it. When was the last time you tried something new? What was that experience like?

_____

_____

_____

_____

_____

_____

_____

_____

_____

_____

_____

_____

_____

_____

_____

_____

Think creatively about new ways to solve old problems.

Your imagination is your mind's ability to form new ideas and create stories without your having had those experiences in real life. Your imagination can allow you to do a variety of things, like plan ahead for stressful experiences so you can cope effectively, repurpose household items to meet your needs, or create a new vision for your life. Your imagination is so powerful that it can even help you be less fearful of things that make you feel anxious. When was the last time you engaged your imagination?

_____

_____

_____

_____

_____

_____

_____

_____

_____

_____

_____

_____

_____

_____

_____

_____

_____

Beginner's mind is a characteristic of mindfulness that focuses on encountering familiar experiences or information as if it were the first time. When you practice beginner's mind, you approach experiences with openness and curiosity, letting go of assumptions and expectations and seeing new possibilities in life. What are some daily activities that have become dull and unexciting? How can you approach those activities with beginner's mind?

_____

_____

_____

_____

_____

_____

_____

_____

_____

_____

_____

_____

_____

Intellectual self-care doesn't have to be strenuous or boring. Think outside the box!

For the following brain teaser (called the nine-dot problem), the goal is to connect all nine dots using only four straight, continuous lines without lifting your pen off the paper. Try to solve the problem in the illustration below without looking up the solution online. As you are working to solve the problem, notice what thoughts and feelings arise. Write them down. What does this exercise teach you about how you respond to intellectual challenges?

●　　　●　　　●

●　　　●　　　●

●　　　●　　　●

_____

_____

_____

_____

_____

_____

_____

_____

_____

_____

_____

With the popularity of the Internet and smartphones, we have an endless supply of online courses at our fingertips. Coursera, Skillshare, and Udemy are some of the most popular online learning platforms. Browse one of these sites and list the top five courses that excite you. Why do you think these courses in particular spoke to you?

_____

_____

_____

_____

_____

_____

_____

_____

_____

_____

_____

_____

_____

_____

Make time for intellectual self-care by replacing some of your idle leisure activities with mentally stimulating tasks.

Dancing can stimulate you physically, emotionally, spiritually, and intellectually. When you learn a new dance routine or style, it challenges your brain to encode the information and store it in your memory. Find a video from YouTube or sign up for a class at your local dance studio, and notice how you are being challenged. Take a moment to reflect on your experience, noting what you enjoyed and what you found challenging.

_____

_____

_____

_____

_____

_____

_____

_____

_____

_____

_____

_____

_____

_____

_____

_____

_____

_____

When our brains are overwhelmed by all the things we need and want to do, it can be hard to concentrate or make progress. A brain dump is decluttering your mind by getting worries, obligations, and to-do lists out of your head and onto your calendar. Do a brain dump right now by writing down all the tasks you need to complete. Then create a plan for how you will get them done.

_____

_____

_____

_____

_____

_____

_____

_____

_____

_____

_____

_____

_____

_____

_____

_____

Reading is self-care for your brain. In what ways can you incorporate more reading into your life? Think creatively. Books are one option, but there are others as well: blogs, magazines, newspapers, and more. Whether you read silently to yourself or to someone else, you'll reap the intellectual benefits.

_____

_____

_____

_____

_____

_____

_____

_____

_____

_____

_____

_____

_____

_____

_____

_____

_____

_____

_____

_____

_____

_____

Writing is a form of intellectual self-care that can help you share your thoughts and think deeply about a specific topic. Try your hand at writing poetry, a story, or a how-to guide about something you know well that other people find challenging.

_____

_____

_____

_____

_____

_____

_____

_____

_____

_____

_____

_____

_____

_____

_____

_____

_____

Take the time to teach others about something you have mastered—this builds your ability to think critically about the topic.

Talking to people who have different opinions on topics we are passionate about can be an act of intellectual self-care. These conversations expose your brain to new ideas, challenging it to think about a familiar topic in a different way. Over the next week, seek out a podcast, news program, social media account, or individual with a viewpoint that's the opposite of yours. Topics could be lighthearted or heavier. What did you learn from exposing yourself to something new?

_____

_____

_____

_____

_____

_____

_____

_____

_____

_____

_____

_____

_____

_____

_____

_____

_____

_____

What do you think about often? Are there any healthy outlets where you could share your thoughts? For example, you could discuss them with friends, start a blog, post on social media, or start a YouTube channel.

_____

_____

_____

_____

_____

_____

_____

_____

_____

_____

_____

_____

_____

_____

_____

_____

When it comes to learning, it can be easy to get caught up in the destination. Be sure to enjoy the journey.

You learn the most when you absorb information in a way that aligns with your learning style. Do you prefer observing or listening? Taking in facts or the theory behind the facts? Trying something hands-on or thinking it through conceptually? The next time you need or want to learn something, how can you set yourself up for success?

The practice of writing down your thoughts and feelings—what you have been doing in this journal—is good for your mind because it helps you make sense of life experiences, notice patterns across time, and express your emotions in a safe and healthy way. Continue your journaling practice by responding to this prompt: The experience that has most impacted me in life is . . .

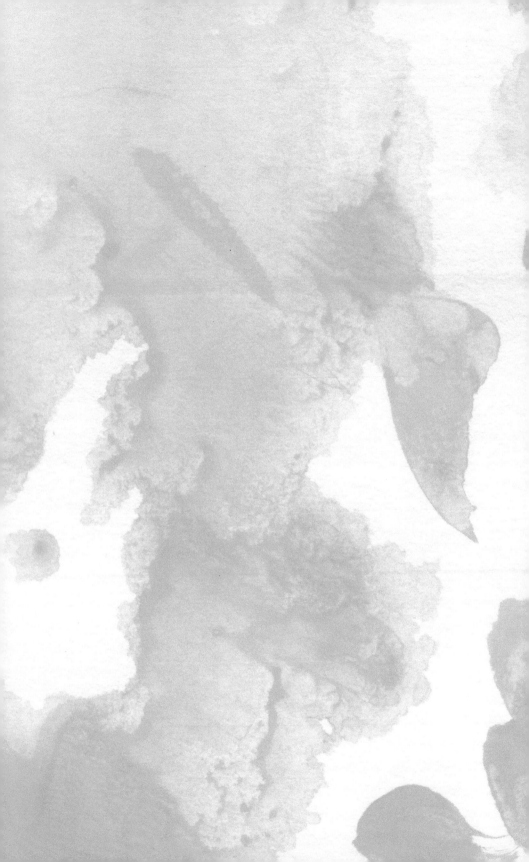

Vocational Self-Care

Humans need meaning and purpose in life. While many people find purpose outside of work, some of us find it in the types of work we choose. Many of us are attracted to work that capitalizes on our natural abilities while allowing us to contribute to a vision larger than ourselves. Vocational self-care involves finding meaning in what you do, using your gifts and talents, connecting with your colleagues and your community, enhancing your satisfaction at work, and creating a balance between your work and personal life.

There are three main components of vocational self-care: career/job, worth, and work/life balance. Self-care in the career/job domain might mean furthering your knowledge in a specific discipline, doing work that feels fulfilling, transitioning to a new job with better pay or benefits, working toward long-term career goals, or taking initiative to create work experiences that are meaningful. In the domain of worth, self-care might involve negotiating pay, taking on additional responsibility, reducing an overwhelming workload, requesting a promotion, or advocating to have a voice in company decisions. In the domain of work/life balance, self-care might look like setting boundaries, prioritizing, or learning to say no.

Although some people are lucky enough to feel fulfilled and satisfied with work, others have jobs they can't stand. The realities of bills, a competitive job market, and family responsibilities make it difficult to simply walk away from a job you dislike. Vocational self-care can make a seemingly intolerable job situation bearable. What's more, when we take care of our vocational needs, we set ourselves up to feel a deeper sense of meaning and purpose in our lives, regardless of our current job status.

What are your gifts, or the skills and abilities, that come naturally to you? Do you use some of them more than others? What, if anything, would you like to change about the way you currently share your talents, skills, and abilities?

Work is most satisfying when it connects to a larger meaning and purpose. Look up your company's vision and mission. Write it down below. What feelings arise as you read these statements? How do you feel about how your specific job tasks contribute to that mission?

_____

_____

_____

_____

_____

_____

_____

_____

_____

_____

_____

_____

_____

_____

_____

_____

Burnout is feeling depleted and overwhelmed by the physical, mental, and emotional demands of work. When we are burned-out, we are less engaged with our work, less productive, and more cynical. Though the best antidote is system-level change, an important buffer against burnout is social connection. When we have colleagues, friends, and family we can turn to for support, we are better able to manage work-related stress. Who can you turn to?

_____

_____

_____

_____

_____

_____

_____

_____

_____

_____

_____

_____

_____

_____

_____

_____

_____

_____

American society views asking for help as a sign of weakness. The popular "pull yourself up by your bootstraps" expectation makes it challenging to ask for help when you are struggling, but doing so is good for your overall health and productivity. What help can you ask for at work?

Ease your workload by asking for help when you need it.

With increasing work responsibilities, it's easy to pack your days full of work activities and meetings. Leaving gaps between appointments and taking brief pauses throughout your day can increase efficiency and reduce exhaustion. How can you create more breaks throughout your workday?

_____

_____

_____

_____

_____

_____

_____

_____

_____

_____

_____

_____

_____

_____

_____

_____

_____

Just like a cell phone that's been unplugged from its power source all day, we need to recharge at the end of the workday. What activities recharge you?

_____

_____

_____

_____

_____

_____

_____

_____

_____

_____

_____

_____

_____

_____

_____

_____

_____

What boundaries have you set between your work and personal life? Do you often find yourself working when you are technically off the clock?

_____

_____

_____

_____

_____

_____

_____

_____

_____

_____

_____

_____

_____

_____

_____

Establish and maintain work/life boundaries by setting specific workdays and/or cutoff times when you will stop working each day.

Do you allow yourself to dream about what is possible for your work, even if it seems impossible? In your wildest dreams, what type of work would you be doing? How would this work contribute to others?

When we find ourselves in less than desirable work circustances, we can keep from making matters worse by maintaining a positive mindset. Focusing on the thought "I hate my job!" just makes the workday longer and dampens your mood. Focus on positive thoughts. If you aspire to a dream job, how can your current job serve as a stepping-stone to your ideal one? What skills can prepare you for that dream career?

_____

_____

_____

_____

_____

_____

_____

_____

_____

_____

_____

_____

_____

_____

_____

_____

_____

_____

What do you want to contribute to the world? What problems or needs are you aware of in your community that you would like to address?

_____

_____

_____

_____

_____

_____

_____

_____

_____

_____

_____

_____

_____

_____

Make the most of your talents, skills, and abilities by applying them outside of your job in volunteer work or other vocational pursuits.

Spending personal time engaged in activities that make you feel competent, confident, and happy can improve your overall quality of life. What hobbies, volunteer work, and recreational activities do you enjoy outside of your paid work? Are there any new ones that you are interested in trying?

_____

_____

_____

_____

_____

_____

_____

_____

_____

_____

_____

_____

_____

_____

_____

_____

_____

_____

Express gratitude for the things your job makes possible, listing all the things it allows you to do. Really think creatively here and allow feelings of thankfulness to flood you as you consider all the things your job makes possible.

_____

_____

_____

_____

_____

_____

_____

_____

_____

_____

_____

_____

_____

_____

_____

_____

_____

_____

Envision your ideal workday. Write out what specific activities you would be engaged in as well as the types of emotions you'd like to experience throughout your day. How can you make your ideal workday (or parts of it) a reality?

_____

_____

_____

_____

_____

_____

_____

_____

_____

_____

_____

_____

_____

_____

_____

_____

_____

_____

_____

_____

Our work can become unfulfilling when we stop learning or are no longer challenged by it. Are you too comfortable with your work? What new challenges can you conquer?

_____

_____

_____

_____

_____

_____

_____

_____

_____

_____

_____

_____

_____

_____

_____

_____

Give yourself healthy challenges in your work life.

We often feel discouraged or unfulfilled in our work because we underestimate our impact. An African proverb says, "If you think you are too small to make a difference, you haven't spent the night with a mosquito." What impact are you making with the work you do? Whose lives are made easier, more efficient, or more enjoyable because of your work?

_____

_____

_____

_____

_____

_____

_____

_____

_____

_____

_____

_____

_____

_____

_____

_____

_____

_____

_____

_____

When you were a child, what did you want to be when you grew up? What about that profession was fascinating to you? Is that profession still of interest to you?

_____

_____

_____

_____

_____

_____

_____

_____

_____

_____

_____

_____

_____

_____

_____

_____

_____

_____

_____

Suppose you won a lifetime achievement award for your work. What type of work and personal qualities would you like to be recognized for during the award presentation? How does the work you do (volunteer or paid) align with the qualities you listed?

_____

_____

_____

_____

_____

_____

_____

_____

_____

_____

_____

_____

_____

_____

_____

_____

_____

Actor Denzel Washington said, "At the end of the day, it's not about what you have or even what you've accomplished. . . . It's about who you've lifted up, who you've made better. It's about what you've given back." In what ways do you give back to your community? How can you establish a deeper connection to your community through volunteer work?

_____

_____

_____

_____

_____

_____

_____

_____

_____

_____

_____

_____

_____

_____

_____

_____

_____

Deriving your identity, value, and sense of self-worth solely from your work can be problematic. When we identify too strongly with the work we do, we can become overly dependent on productivity, achievement, and accolades for our happiness. Who are you outside of the work titles and academic degrees you have earned?

_____

_____

_____

_____

_____

_____

_____

_____

_____

_____

_____

_____

_____

_____

Unravel your identity from the work you do. You are more than your work. Remember who you are beyond the work you do.

What is your biggest challenge in your work? Are these challenges something that you have control over? What actions can you take to cope more effectively with your work-related challenges?

_____

_____

_____

_____

_____

_____

_____

_____

_____

_____

_____

_____

_____

_____

_____

_____

_____

_____

_____

What gives you the energy you need to do the work you do? Consider both physical and emotional energy. Monitor your energy levels throughout your workday over the next week. What self-care activities increase your energy? What activities or people drain your energy?

_____

_____

_____

_____

_____

_____

_____

_____

_____

_____

_____

_____

_____

_____

_____

_____

_____

_____

_____

It's been said, "Comparison is the thief of joy." We are more prone to dissatisfaction in our work when we compare ourselves to others. Competing with coworkers is a recipe for disappointment and unhappiness. When it comes your education and career, do you compare yourself to others? What practical steps can you take to let go of comparison?

_____

_____

_____

_____

_____

_____

_____

_____

_____

_____

_____

_____

Take stock of what depletes and replenishes your energy. Increase energy-giving activities and relationships, and let go of energy-draining activities and relationships.

What mindset and attitudes do you bring to your work? When you face difficulties or challenges at work, are you more of a glass-half-empty or glass-half-full person? How does this mindset serve you? How does it work against you?

_____

_____

_____

_____

_____

_____

_____

_____

_____

_____

_____

_____

_____

_____

_____

_____

_____

_____

_____

Unhappiness results when we spend our lives striving to attain someone else's definition of success. What is your definition of success? Have you ever found yourself making vocational choices that are misaligned with your heart's desires? What is the next step you can take toward your personal definition of success?

_____

_____

_____

_____

_____

_____

_____

_____

_____

_____

_____

_____

_____

_____

Monitor your mindset and make necessary shifts to improve your mood while at work.

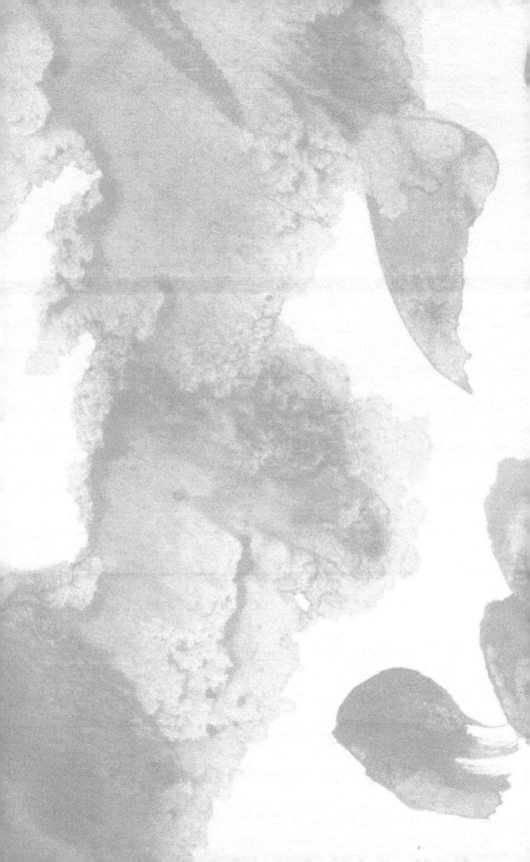

Spiritual Self-Care

Beyond what you see when you look in the mirror and all the labels and titles you've been assigned, at your core, there is a spirit. The energy you bring into a room, the values and beliefs you use to guide your life choices, the inner drive you have for purpose and meaning—this is your spirit, your soul.

Spiritual self-care is about nurturing your soul, slowing down, and turning your attention inward. Tending to your spirit gives you meaning, perspective, hope, and clarity. It naturally involves connection with something larger than yourself, and with others who are on the same path. Without conscious effort to turn your attention inward on a regular basis, you risk being flooded with anxiety and worry. When you prioritize spiritual self-care, you can experience gratitude, peace, contentment, and joy. Spiritual practices can lower depression, increase life satisfaction, facilitate adjustment after trauma, induce calmer and more positive attitudes during illnesses, and help you more effectively manage stress.

There is no one right way to tend to your spirit. For some, spiritual self-care means involvement in organized religion. For others, it involves practicing yoga or meditation, journaling, connecting with nature, clearing the chakras, or serving the community. There are three main components to spiritual self-care: faith, community, and humanity. Faith means having confidence and hope in things you cannot see. Community means stepping out of yourself and joining with others who care for you. Humanity means taking steps to be nonjudgmental, addressing your unconscious bias, and using your power and privilege to be an advocate for people who are marginalized. Faith, community, and humanity can enrich your life by helping you navigate challenging times, look forward to the future, and make sense of the things you go through.

What five words best describe your spiritual values? How do you embody these qualities in daily life? If you do not have spiritual values or practices, write down what you believe about the way the world works. For example, how do you make sense of things that seem bizarre, unfair, or unjust?

_____

_____

_____

_____

_____

_____

_____

_____

_____

_____

_____

_____

_____

_____

_____

_____

_____

_____

To nurture your spirit, it's important to have an idea of what you need spiritually. Take a moment to sit still. Close your eyes and say quietly to yourself: "My spirit needs." Wait patiently for the response. Write down the responses that come to you.

_____

_____

_____

_____

_____

_____

_____

_____

_____

_____

_____

_____

_____

_____

_____

_____

_____

Our souls can be nourished by connecting to something larger than us or something inspiring, like a quote or a hopeful song. When was the last time your soul felt nourished? What actions can you take to nourish it more? When you refill your spirit, you can give to others from the overflow.

_____

_____

_____

_____

_____

_____

_____

_____

_____

_____

_____

_____

_____

_____

_____

_____

Create time for spiritual care by delegating tasks that don't require your skill or expertise.

What experiences have been the most pivotal to you becoming the person you are today?

_____

_____

_____

_____

_____

_____

_____

_____

_____

_____

_____

_____

_____

_____

_____

_____

_____

_____

_____

_____

It's okay to love and appreciate the person you are today while journeying toward your goals. How can you show yourself genuine love and appreciation while you are on the path to becoming the person you want to be?

_____

_____

_____

_____

_____

_____

_____

_____

_____

_____

_____

_____

_____

_____

_____

_____

_____

_____

_____

Faith is believing in what we can't see. What do you have faith in?

_____

_____

_____

_____

_____

_____

_____

_____

_____

_____

_____

_____

_____

_____

_____

_____

_____

_____

With so many things on our plates, we are vulnerable to feeling overwhelmed and anxious, causing our thoughts to race and our spirits to become uneasy and restless. What are some things you can do to calm your mind and keep a positive mindset when you feel overwhelmed?

_____

_____

_____

_____

_____

_____

_____

_____

_____

_____

_____

_____

_____

_____

_____

Light your favorite scented candle or warm an essential oil. Aromatherapy can bring a sense of peace and calm when life seems chaotic.

Paul Laurence Dunbar's poem "We Wear the Mask" describes various ways that we hide our thoughts and feelings to make other people comfortable. What thoughts and feelings are hidden behind your mask? What is the cost of wearing your mask? What would it feel like to unmask yourself?

Barack Obama said, "Change will not come if we wait for some other person or some other time. We are the ones we've been waiting for. We are the change that we seek." What change have you been waiting for? How might you be the change that you seek?

_____

_____

_____

_____

_____

_____

_____

_____

_____

_____

_____

_____

_____

_____

_____

_____

_____

_____

What does peace feel like? When you are overwhelmed, what spiritual practices bring you peace? What actions can you take to protect your peace?

_____

_____

_____

_____

_____

_____

_____

_____

_____

_____

_____

_____

_____

_____

_____

_____

_____

_____

In today's society, we are constantly bombarded with the beliefs and opinions of others. It's easy to feel disconnected from your truth, what's most important and meaningful to you. When you quiet the external noise, what truth is present?

_____

_____

_____

_____

_____

_____

_____

_____

_____

_____

_____

_____

_____

_____

_____

_____

_____

_____

Offer yourself one small act of kindness each day. It can be as small as a smile at yourself in the mirror. You get to decide!

Hustling is one way to live, but it's not the only way. We can make progress toward becoming the people we want to become without rushing, setting unrealistic expectations, and placing excessive pressure on ourselves. How would your days be different if you embraced the journey and let go of the hustle?

_____

_____

_____

_____

_____

_____

_____

_____

_____

_____

_____

_____

_____

_____

_____

_____

_____

_____

_____

_____

What spiritual place, thing, or person do you feel connected to?

_____

_____

_____

_____

_____

_____

_____

_____

_____

_____

_____

_____

_____

_____

_____

_____

_____

_____

_____

_____

_____

Our legacies are the footprints we leave on Earth. What legacy are you creating? How do you want to be remembered?

_____

_____

_____

_____

_____

_____

_____

_____

_____

_____

_____

_____

_____

_____

_____

_____

_____

_____

What encouragement does your heart most need to hear? Can you offer those words to yourself as an act of self-love and generosity?

_____

_____

_____

_____

_____

_____

_____

_____

_____

_____

_____

_____

_____

_____

_____

_____

_____

_____

_____

_____

_____

Your intuition is like a compass that guides you in the direction of what matters most to you. Which best characterizes your relationship with your intuition: strangers, acquaintances, or best friends? What gets in the way of you hearing from your higher self?

_____

_____

_____

_____

_____

_____

_____

_____

_____

_____

_____

_____

_____

_____

_____

_____

_____

_____

_____

_____

_____

What communities do you feel most connected to? What actions can you take to more regularly connect with communities that share your spiritual values and practices?

_____

_____

_____

_____

_____

_____

_____

_____

_____

_____

_____

_____

_____

_____

_____

_____

_____

_____

_____

_____

By showing up in the world as the full version of ourselves, we create the possibility to feel truly seen, valued, and respected. What people and spaces allow you to show up as your full self?

_____

_____

_____

_____

_____

_____

_____

_____

_____

_____

_____

_____

_____

_____

Join or create groups where you can regularly get together with people with similar spiritual values and share what's on your heart and mind.

What quote, proverb, poem, song lyric, or scripture gives you hope? Why?

_____

_____

_____

_____

_____

_____

_____

_____

_____

_____

_____

_____

_____

_____

_____

_____

_____

_____

_____

_____

_____

The challenges we face in life can keep us from seeing ourselves clearly. In what ways have you been labeled or defined by negative life experiences?

_____

_____

_____

_____

_____

_____

_____

_____

_____

_____

_____

_____

_____

_____

_____

_____

_____

We can feed our spirits through the arts.
Recite your favorite lyric, scripture, poem,
quote, or proverb to lift your spirits.

To transcend our personal experiences means to rise above them. We transcend difficulties when we thrive despite them. What negative experiences in life have you transcended? What lessons have you learned from adversity?

_____

_____

_____

_____

_____

_____

_____

_____

_____

_____

_____

_____

_____

_____

_____

_____

_____

_____

When we have faced rejection and disappointments in life, hope can feel risky. How have past hurtful experiences affected your willingness to hope? What hopes would you like to revive?

_____

_____

_____

_____

_____

_____

_____

_____

_____

_____

_____

_____

_____

_____

_____

_____

_____

_____

In some faiths, followers are called to be lights of the world. Light provides clarity, hope, and guidance. What ways do you bring light into the world?

_____

_____

_____

_____

_____

_____

_____

_____

_____

_____

_____

_____

_____

_____

_____

_____

_____

_____

_____

Our souls are troubled when we try to regulate things beyond our control. Where can you release control in your life?

_____

_____

_____

_____

_____

_____

_____

_____

_____

_____

_____

_____

_____

_____

_____

Sometimes we multitask out of habit, not necessity. Practice noticing when multitasking isn't truly needed. Allow yourself to do one thing at a time.

What power and privileges do you enjoy due to your gender identity, ethnicity, age, body size, ability standing, financial standing, or immigration status? What assumptions do you make about people who are less privileged? How do these assumptions affect the way you feel spiritually?

_____

_____

_____

_____

_____

_____

_____

_____

_____

_____

_____

_____

_____

_____

_____

_____

_____

_____

_____

_____

When the trials of life get too heavy to bear, it can be helpful to remember you are spiritually connected to others who have done hard things. The same persistence, courage, and fight that allowed your ancestors to overcome their struggles is available to you. Who are your ancestors? How can you connect to their wisdom and strength in times of difficulty?

_____

_____

_____

_____

_____

_____

_____

_____

_____

_____

_____

_____

_____

_____

_____

Challenge yourself to think of ways that obstacles can be opportunities for growth.

Emotional Self-Care

While many of us welcome pleasurable emotions, we get into trouble in managing the not-so-pleasurable ones. As humans, we're bound to experience sorrow, fear, disappointment, shame, and anger. There's no getting around it; these emotions are normal and inevitable. The key to our emotional health is how we cope with those emotions.

"The Guest House," a poem by Rumi, compares the various emotions we experience to uninvited houseguests. It suggests we treat our emotions as we would any guest who visited our home, even if they aren't our favorite person in the world. Although the guest may be obnoxious or inconsiderate, we acknowledge their presence, welcome them, and treat them with respect because we are polite and hospitable. This is the type of relationship we want to cultivate with all of our emotions.

Emotional self-care is about labeling and recognizing our emotions, knowing our triggers, and having the skills and tools to cope with them. Emotions are messengers that alert us to things that need our attention. Emotional self-care invites us to accept our emotions as they are rather than ignoring, numbing, or avoiding them. When we take care of ourselves emotionally, we are willing to sit with our emotions, learn from them, and, when necessary, work through them. When we are emotionally aware and well, we can handle stress effectively and heal from trauma. Emotional self-care practices like gratitude can help us be thankful for our blessings, see the silver lining when life's challenges come our way, and realize that no matter how difficult an emotion may feel, it won't last forever. Emotional self-care helps us tap into this truth of our emotional experience.

Reflect on the social media pages you follow. Which pages make you feel good? Which ones make you feel bad or inadequate in some way? Unfollowing pages that make you feel bad about yourself is an act of self-care.

_____

_____

_____

_____

_____

_____

_____

_____

_____

_____

_____

_____

_____

_____

_____

_____

When consuming news, social media, and films,
pay attention to how they make you feel.

It's important to have emotional outlets. Verbally communicating your emotions is one way to express them. You can also express them creatively through the arts—dance/performance, music, literature, film, social media content, painting, and sculpture. Choose a method of artistic expression and use it to process an emotion you have been experiencing a lot lately.

_____

_____

_____

_____

_____

_____

_____

_____

_____

_____

_____

_____

_____

_____

_____

_____

_____

Avoiding, stuffing, or numbing emotions creates more emotional pain in the long run. When we sit with our emotions, no matter how painful they are, we can then receive the information they came to teach and develop healthy ways of expressing and coping with them. What emotion(s) would you like to learn to sit with? How do you imagine sitting with them will benefit you?

Emotion regulation is the ability to influence our emotions. It allows us to decrease or increase the intensity of our emotions and control how we respond to them. How do you manage pleasant and unpleasant emotions? What are your typical emotion regulation strategies?

Typically, when we think about grief and loss, the death of someone comes to mind. However, there are other types of loss, like the loss of a dream, a friendship, a partner through divorce, or a physical ability due to illness. What losses have affected you the most? Have you allowed yourself to grieve?

_____

_____

_____

_____

_____

_____

_____

_____

_____

_____

_____

_____

_____

_____

_____

_____

_____

Emotional triggers are events, experiences, or topics that evoke strong, uncomfortable emotions. How do you take care of yourself when you have been emotionally triggered?

_____

_____

_____

_____

_____

_____

_____

_____

_____

_____

_____

_____

_____

_____

_____

_____

Identifying the thoughts and events that trigger emotions provides the clarity and guidance needed to cope effectively.

Self-compassion is the practice of treating ourselves with kindness when we are experiencing painful emotions. It's caring for yourself the same way you would comfort a toddler who falls while learning how to walk. If I could listen to your internal dialogue, what would I hear? How do you treat yourself when you make a mistake or fall short of your expectations? What can you do today to offer yourself more kindness and compassion?

Vulnerability is hard, especially when our trust has been betrayed or we have been abandoned or rejected in the past. It is a risk and there are no certain outcomes, but vulnerability also helps us feel more connected in our relationships. What have you given up on because of past trauma, rejection, or loss? What would be possible for you if you risked making yourself vulnerable?

_____

_____

_____

_____

_____

_____

_____

_____

_____

_____

_____

_____

_____

_____

_____

_____

In an approach called dialectical behavior therapy, clients are taught four skills in order to calm down when their emotions are boiling over: do something to change your body temperature (e.g., take a cold shower), get your heart pumping with intense exercise, take slow deep belly breaths, and systematically squeeze then release all the major muscle groups in your body. Of these four skills, which do you think could be most beneficial to you the next time your emotions feel out of your control?

_____

_____

_____

_____

_____

_____

_____

_____

_____

_____

_____

_____

_____

_____

_____

_____

_____

Brené Brown said, "When we deny our stories, they define us. When we own our stories, we can write a brave new ending." What story do you need to own?

_____

_____

_____

_____

_____

_____

_____

_____

_____

_____

_____

_____

_____

_____

_____

_____

_____

_____

Gratitude can increase happiness and resilience as well as reduce anxiety, stress, and risk of depression. It doesn't always come easy but is a skill we can build that become effortless with practice. For the next week, try writing down three things you are grateful for each day. Using a 0–10 scale, where 0 is not at all happy and 10 is extremely happy, rate your happiness at the beginning of the week then again at the end of the week. How was your overall mood and happiness affected by this practice?

Happiness Rating #1: ___

Day 1

I am grateful for:

_____

_____

_____

Day 2

I am grateful for:

_____

_____

_____

Day 3

I am grateful for:

_____

_____

_____

Day 4

I am grateful for:

_____

_____

_____

Day 5

I am grateful for:

_____

_____

_____

Day 6

I am grateful for:

_____

_____

_____

Day 7

I am grateful for:

_____

_____

_____

Happiness Rating #2: ___

Self-soothing is offering your body comfort, loving care, and attention when you are experiencing challenging emotions. One of the easiest access points to soothing the body is through the five senses: sight, touch, smell, sound, and taste. Which of the five senses most appeals to you? How might you use this sense to soothe yourself when you need nurturing?

_____

_____

_____

_____

_____

_____

_____

_____

_____

_____

_____

_____

When we are in emotional pain, our impulse is to rush and get rid of the emotion. Often, a better response is to ask, "What do I need right now?"

Sometimes, unpleasant emotions are triggered by neglecting basic needs, like food, sleep, and movement. The next time you notice you are feeling an unpleasant emotion, check in with yourself to see whether a basic need needs to be fulfilled. Regularly fulfilling these needs helps us better manage stress, decreases our vulnerability to intense emotion, and makes us less likely to act impulsively when we are emotionally over-whelmed. Which basic needs are you most prone to neglect? What actions can you take to better meet them?

_____

_____

_____

_____

_____

_____

_____

_____

_____

_____

_____

_____

_____

_____

_____

Nearly 70 percent of people experience something traumatic during their lifetime. We also have inherited ancestral traumas from our lineage. What traumas have you been exposed to both personally and ancestrally? How have you healed from trauma and what healing work remains?

_____

_____

_____

_____

_____

_____

_____

_____

_____

_____

_____

_____

_____

_____

_____

_____

_____

_____

_____

_____

As complex humans, we rarely feel just one emotion at a time. Sometimes contradictory emotions arise at the same time (e.g., joy and fear, connection and uncertainty, sadness and pride). We cause ourselves more emotional pain when we try to force our emotional experience to be one-dimensional. Have you ever had the experience of conflicting emotions arising at the same time? What would it look like to honor and fully accept all of your emotions?

_____

_____

_____

_____

_____

_____

_____

_____

_____

_____

_____

_____

_____

_____

Take small steps to create the relationship you want to have with your emotions.

Our emotions are not problems that need to be solved. They are signals, gentle messengers alerting us that something needs our attention. Often, what we most need when we experience painful emotions is to be seen, heard, and held rather than fixed. What people in your life allow you to just be without trying to fix or solve your emotions? How can you offer yourself the gift of truly seeing, hearing, and holding yourself in the midst of your emotions?

_____

_____

_____

_____

_____

_____

_____

_____

_____

_____

_____

_____

_____

_____

_____

_____

_____

Fear is a normal emotion when you are pursuing a goal, doing something new or challenging, or taking a risk. We become stuck in our lives when we are unwilling to feel uncomfortable, and invest too much energy in trying to avoid feeling afraid. If you wait for fear to go away before you begin something, you'll likely never start. What have you been waiting to do until you no longer feel afraid? What would it be like to stop waiting and do it even though you are afraid?

_____

_____

_____

_____

_____

_____

_____

_____

_____

_____

_____

_____

_____

_____

_____

_____

You have the ability to create the emotions you want to experience. We create emotional experiences for ourselves through our actions, the attitudes we cultivate, and the thoughts we choose to focus on. List three to five emotions you want to experience. When have you experienced these emotions in the past? What thoughts, actions, and habits would you need to create the emotional experiences you desire?

_____

_____

_____

_____

_____

_____

_____

_____

_____

_____

_____

_____

_____

_____

It can be easy to focus on what we don't want. Challenge yourself to focus on what you do want.

Many people identify anger as one of the most challenging emotions. It's hard to transform an emotion when you are aren't aware of the underlying cause. Anger is a secondary emotion. Secondary emotions arise to protect us from more vulnerable, painful emotions like fear and sadness. Reflect on the last time you were angry by answering the following questions: What was I afraid of? What sadness was underneath my anger? The next time you feel angry, you can ask yourself these same questions.

Validating our emotions is key to coping with them in healthy ways. When you validate an emotion, you label it and allow yourself to feel it. You tell yourself how it makes sense based on the event that triggered it and resist the urge to judge yourself for feeling the way you do. How are you feeling right now? It may be helpful to close your eyes and observe your body to get a clear sense of how you are feeling. Practice validating your emotion. What was the experience like? What did emotional validation create space for?

_____

_____

_____

_____

_____

_____

_____

_____

_____

_____

_____

_____

_____

_____

_____

_____

Painful emotions come on fast and furious. Catching us off guard, they can hijack even the best of days. Emotions are often triggered by experiences or by thoughts, but nailing down the specific cause can be difficult when we are flooded with emotion. When you want to understand the cause of an emotion, take a deep breath and ask yourself, "What experience or thought triggered this emotion?"

_____

_____

_____

_____

_____

_____

_____

_____

_____

_____

_____

_____

_____

_____

_____

_____

When we struggle with comparison, jealousy, or envy, the root of it is a story we've been telling ourselves about who we are, what we lack, or what we aren't capable of. What narrative have you been telling yourself about who you are and what's possible for you? Where did it come from? How can you create a new one?

_____

_____

_____

_____

_____

_____

_____

_____

_____

_____

_____

_____

_____

_____

_____

_____

_____

_____

A Final Reflection

We have reached the end of our journey together. Thank you for showing up for yourself and devoting time to your self-care. Self-care isn't always pleasant, but it is worth the effort. The better you know yourself, the more equipped you are to fulfill your self-care needs. I hope this journal is just one small—but meaningful—part of a lifelong self-care journey. As you move forward, remember that you are a full human with physical, emotional, spiritual, social, vocational, and intellectual needs. These needs deserve to be fulfilled from a place of self-love, intentionality, and honor.

Hopefully, this journal has helped you to see that self-care is so much more than the glamorous, commercialized images we see on TV and social media. Real self-care doesn't require countless hours and lots of money, and it's not just another item on your to-do list. Keep in mind, there is no one right way to take care of yourself. Just as the seasons change, so will your self-care needs. What is best for you today may not be what you need next week (or next year), and that's okay. The most important thing is to stay in touch with yourself. Take time on a regular basis to be still and listen to what your heart, mind, body, and soul are whispering to you. The answer is always there; you just have to be willing to listen and then take inspired action. When the demands of this world try pulling you in a million different directions, I hope the things you wrote down in this journal will remind you of what truly matters.

As you continue working toward building the world we envisioned together at the beginning of this journal, remember this: Self-care is not selfish, and it's not a luxury. Self-care is your birthright. Walk unapologetically in this truth.

Resources

Websites/Podcasts/Social Media Accounts

The Nap Ministry (Instagram.com/thenapministry): a social justice movement that uses performance art to highlight the liberating power of naps

Therapy for Black Girls (TherapyForBlackGirls.com): a podcast, online community, and directory designed to support mental wellness and make mental health relevant and accessible for Black women

Psychologists Off the Clock (OffTheClockPsych.com): a podcast that applies psychology principles to help you flourish in work and life

National Alliance on Mental Illness (NAMI.org): a grassroots organization that offers information about mental illness and advocates on behalf of individuals who are affected by it

Apps and Blogs

Shine: a meditation app that supports emotional and spiritual self-care

Liberate: a meditation app designed to support overall wellness among BIPOC

ThinkUp: an affirmation app that can support every area of self-care

Proverbs 31 Ministries: a nondenominational, nonprofit Christian ministry that promotes spiritual wellness among women and offers online Bible studies

Books

The Self-Care Prescription: Powerful Solutions to Manage Stress, Reduce Anxiety & Increase Wellbeing by Robyn L. Gobin: the self-care book this journal was based on

The Body Is Not an Apology: The Power of Radical Self-Love by Sonya Renee Taylor: a book designed to help you love and embrace yourself just as you are

The Big Leap: Conquer Your Hidden Fear and Take Life to the Next Level by Gay Hendricks: a book designed to equip you with practical tools for conquering your fears and pursuing your dreams in life

It's About Time: The Art of Choosing the Meaningful Over the Urgent by Valorie Burton: a book that will show you how to invest your precious time in what matters most

References

Social Self-Care

Angelou, Maya. Twitter, September 2, 2018. Twitter.com/DrMayaAngelou/status/1036327789488734208.

Brown, Brené *Daring Greatly: How the Courage to Be Vulnerable Transforms the Way We Live, Love, Parent, and Lead.* New York: Penguin, 2015.

Holt-Lunstad, J., T. F. Robles, and D. A. Sbarra. "Advancing Social Connection as a Public Health Priority in the United States." *American Psychologist* 72, no. 6 (2017): 517–30.

Greater Good Magazine. "Forgiveness Defined." Accessed October 20, 2020. GreaterGood.Berkeley.edu/topic/forgiveness/definition.

Physical Self-Care

Cross, K. "Comfort in Clothing: Fashion Actors and Victims." Paper presented at 21st International Foundation of Fashion Technology Institute Conference, Manchester, UK, April 2019. FashionInstitute.MMU.ac.uk/ifftipapers/paper-168.

Cuddy, Amy. *Presence: Bringing Your Boldest Self to Your Biggest Challenges.* New York: Little, Brown and Company, 2015.

Dalton-Smith, Saundra. "The Real Reason Why We Are Tired and What to Do about It." TEDx Talks. Filmed April 9, 2019 in Atlanta, GA. YouTube video, 09:34. YouTube.com/watch?v=ZGNN4EPJzGk.

Dalton-Smith, Saundra. *Sacred Rest: Recover Your Life, Renew Your Energy, Restore Your Sanity.* New York: FaithWords, 2019.

Griffiths, Kadeen. "Shonda Rhimes Encourages Us to Change the World." Bustle. November 10, 2016. Bustle.com/articles/194672-shonda-rhimes-has -amessage-that-every-woman-needs-to-hear-right-now.

Hoffman, K. M., S. Trawalter, J. R. Axt, and M. N. Oliver. "Racial Bias in Pain Assessment and Treatment Recommendations, and False Beliefs about Biological Differences between Blacks and Whites." *PNAS* 113, no. 16 (2016): 4296–301. DOI.org/10.1073/pnas.1516047113.

Marcelin, J. R., D. S. Siraj, R. Victor, S. Kotadia, and Y. A. Maldonado. "The Impact of Unconscious Bias in Healthcare: How to Recognize and Mitigate It." *Journal of Infectious Diseases* 220, no. 2 (2019): S62-73.

Mayo Clinic. "Exercise: 7 Benefits of Regular Physical Activity." May 11, 2019. MayoClinic.org/healthy-lifestyle/fitness/in-depth/exercise/art-20048389.

Medina, Clifford. "How Often Should You Get a Check-up?" Mount Sinai Medical Center. Last modified October 7, 2020. MSMC.com/how-often -should-you-get-a-check-up.

Tesema, Martha. "A Beginner's Guide to Taking Up Space." Shine. July 20, 2020. Advice.TheShineApp.com/articles/a-beginners-guide-to-taking-up -space.

Watson, N. F., M. S. Badr, G. Belenky, D. L. Bliwise, O. M. Buxton, D. Buysse, D. F. Dinges, et al. "Recommended Amount of Sleep for a Healthy Adult: A Joint Consensus Statement of the American Academy of Sleep Medicine and Sleep Research Society." *Journal of Clinical Sleep Medicine* 11, no. 6 (2015): 591–92. DOI.org/10.5664/jcsm.4758.

Xu J., S. L. Murphy, K. D. Kochanek, and E. Arias. *Mortality in the United States, 2018.* NCHS Data Brief, no. 355. Hyattsville, MD: National Center for Health Statistics, 2020. CDC.gov/nchs/products/databriefs/db355.htm.

Intellectual Self-Care

Burton, C. M., and L. A. King. "The Health Benefits of Writing about Intensely Positive Experiences." *Journal of Research in Personality* 38, no. 2 (2004): 150–63.

Galli, G., M. Sirota, M. J. Gruber, B. E. Ivanof, J. Ganesh, M. Materassi, A. Thorpe, et al. "Learning Facts during Aging: The Benefits of Curiosity." *Experimental Aging Research* 44, no. 4 (2018): 311–28. DOI.org/10.1080/0361 073X.2018.1477355.

Kabat-Zinn, Jon, and Hanh, Thich Nhat. *Full Catastrophe Living: Using the Wisdom of Your Body and Mind to Face Stress, Pain, and Illness.* New York: Random House, 2009.

Kershaw, Trina C., and Stellan Ohlsson. "Training for Insight: The Case of the Nine-Dot Problem." University of Illinois at Chicago, Department of Psychology. Accessed November 3, 2020. Conferences.inf.ed.ac.uk/cogsci2001/pdf-files/0489.pdf.

Maier, N. R. F. "Reasoning in humans. I. On direction." *Journal of Comparative Psychology* 10, no. 2 (1930): 115–43. DOI.org/10.1037/h0073232.

Mental Floss. "6 Proven Benefits of Being More Imaginative." Accessed November 3, 2020. MentalFloss.com/article/517642/6-proven-benefits-being-more-imaginative.

Qian, J., X. Zhou, X. Sun, M. Wu, S. Sun, and X. Yu. "Effects of Expressive Writing Intervention for Women's PTSD, Depression, Anxiety and Stress Related to Pregnancy: A Meta-Analysis of Randomized Controlled Trials." *Psychiatry Research* 288 (2020): 112933.

Reddan, M. C., T. D. Wager, and D. Schiller. "Attenuating Neural Threat Expression with Imagination." *Neuron* 100, no. 4 (2018): 994–1005.

ScienceDaily. "How Walking Benefits the Brain: Researchers Show That Foot's Impact Helps Control, Increase the Amount of Blood Sent to the Brain." Accessed November 3, 2020. ScienceDaily.com/releases/2017/04/170424141340.htm.

Sloan, D. M., B. P. Marx, P. A. Resick, S. Young-McCaughan, K. A. Dondanville, J. Mintz, B. Litz, et al. "Study Design Comparing Written Exposure Therapy to Cognitive Processing Therapy for PTSD among Military Service Members: A Noninferiority Trial." *Contemporary Clinical Trials Communications* 17 (2020): 100507.

Vocational Self-Care

Haber, M. A., G. C. Gaviola, J. R. Mann, J. Kim, F. E. Malone, S. A. Matalon, S. Chikarmane, et al. "Reducing Burnout among Radiology Trainees: A Novel Residency Retreat Curriculum to Improve Camaraderie and Personal Wellness—3 Strategies for Success." *Current Problems in Diagnostic Radiology* 49, no. 2 (2020): 89–95.

Valcour, Monique. "Beating Burnout." *Harvard Business Review*. November 2016. HBR.org/2016/11/beating-burnout.

Washington, Denzel. *A Hand to Guide Me*. Des Moines: Meredith Books, 2006.

Spiritual Self-Care

Labbé, E. E., and A. Fobes. "Evaluating the Interplay between Spirituality, Personality and Stress." *Applied Psychophysiology and Biofeedback* 35, no. 2 (2010): 141–46.

Lifshitz, R., G. Nimrod, and Y. G. Bachner. "Spirituality and Wellbeing in Later Life: A Multidimensional Approach." *Aging & Mental Health* 23, no. 8 (2019): 984–91.

New York Times. "Barack Obama's Feb. 5 Speech." February 5, 2008. NYTimes.com/2008/02/05/us/politics/05text-obama.html.

Park, C. L. "Spiritual Well-Being after Trauma: Correlates with Appraisals, Coping, and Psychological Adjustment." *Journal of Prevention & Intervention in the Community* 45, no. 4 (2017): 297–307.

Toledo, G., C. Y. Ochoa, and A. J. Farias. "Religion and Spirituality: Their Role in the Psychosocial Adjustment to Breast Cancer and Subsequent Symptom Management of Adjuvant Endocrine Therapy." *Supportive Care in Cancer* (2020): 1–8. DOI.org/10.1007/s00520-020-05722-4.

Emotional Self-Care

Benjet C., E. Bromet, E. G. Karam, R. C. Kessler, K. A. McLaughlin, A. M. Ruscio, V. Shahly, et al. "The Epidemiology of Traumatic Event Exposure Worldwide: Results from the World Mental Health Survey Consortium." *Psychological Medicine* 46, no. 2 (2016): 327–43. DOI.org/10.1017/S0033291715001981.

Blabst, N., and S. Diefenbach. "New Forms of Recording Gratitude: Benefits of a Gratitude Journal App and an Exploration of Appreciated Design Features." *European Journal of Applied Positive Psychology* 2, no. 2 (2018): 1–11.

Brown, Brené. "Own Our History. Change the Story." June 18, 2015. BreneBrown.com/blog/2015/06/18/own-o ur-history-change-the-story.

Harris, Russ. *The Happiness Trap: How to Stop Struggling and Start Living*. Boston: Trumpeter Books, 2008.

Kessler, R. C., A. Sonnega, E. Bromet, M. Hughes, and C. B. Nelson. "Posttraumatic stress disorder in the National Comorbidity Survey." *Archives of General Psychiatry* 52, no. 12 (1995): 1048-60.

Kilpatrick, D. G., H. S. Resnick, M. E. Milanak, M. W. Miller, K. M. Keyes, and M. J. Friedman. "National Estimates of Exposure to Traumatic Events and PTSD Prevalence Using DSM-IV and DSM-5 Criteria." *Journal of Traumatic Stress* 26, no. 5 (2013): 537–47.

Linehan, Marsha. *DBT Skills Training Manual*. New York: Guilford Publications, 2015.

Wood, A. M., J. J. Froh, and A. W. Geraghty. "Gratitude and Well-being: A Review and Theoretical Integration." *Clinical Psychology Review* 30, no. 7 (2010): 890–905.

About the Author

Robyn L. Gobin, PhD, is a licensed clinical psychologist, mindfulness teacher, speaker, researcher, and university professor. Dr. Gobin is dedicated to helping others improve their lives by taking inspired action, managing their mindset, and embracing their worth. In her free time, she enjoys snuggling on the couch with her family for movie night, shopping, practicing restorative yoga, reading for spiritual nourishment, and trying new recipes.

CPSIA information can be obtained
at www.ICGtesting.com
Printed in the USA
JSHW011859170622
26945JS00002B/5